For Malcolm
with best wish
Diana Bro

# DRAWING THE LINE

## AND OTHER POEMS

# DRAWING THE LINE

## AND OTHER POEMS

### BY

### DIANA BISHOP

## THE BREWSTER PRESS

STANHOE, KING'S LYNN, NORFOLK

2012

Published 2012 by The Brewster Press
Stanhoe, King's Lynn, Norfolk PE31 8QD
Tel: (01485) 518 232
www.thebrewsterpress.com
E-mail: info@thebrewsterpress.com

Reprinted 2013

Typeset in Sylfaen 11 point

Photograph of Diana Bishop by Claire Grogan

Photograph on page 79 by courtesy of
Antoine Soto, Brussels

Printed and bound in the UK
by the MPG Books Group, Bodmin and King's Lynn

ISBN 978-0-9572790-0-1

*For my father*

*who always knew the meanings of words*

*and*

*with love to my husband Alan,*

*to Greg and Abbie*

*and to Jean*

*and all my families*

# Also by Diana Bishop

*The Enchanted Cave*
*Leonardo — A Life Well Used*

Adaptation of and Lyrics for
*The Secret Garden*
with music by Alan Mason

Poems and Lyrics for
*Here's Looking at You*
with music by Alan Mason

For the BBC:

plays including
*The Rest of Heaven was Blue*
*Errors of the Past*
*Sing Until Tomorrow*

and

short stories including
*The Fur Coat*
*Eating Grapes Downwards*
*Grandmother's Footsteps*

# Acknowledgements

My thanks to the editors of the following magazines and anthologies where some of these poems were first published: *Envoi Magazine, Kites Anthology, The Rada Poets, The South Bank Poetry Magazine,* and *Poetry Review.*

Also to Michael Bell of *The Brewster Press* for his time, patience and good company.

*Visiting Rousseau* was awarded First Prize by the London Regional Arts Club in 1978

*Small Protests* won First Prize at the Lancaster Literary Festival in 1980

*Amour Propre 1926* won First Prize at the 1981 Honey Magazine Competition

*To My Daughter* was awarded a Commendation at the Ver Poets Open Competition 1981

*Most of Us* won First Prize at the 1982 Poets for Peace Competition

*Famous Photograph* received a Commendation at the 1992 Barnet Open Competition

*Man Marks the Earth* received an Honourable Mention at the 1997 Wildlife Poet of the Year Competition

*Felled* won Second Prize at the 2000 Barnet Open Competition

*Alone* received a High Commendation at the Ver Poets Open Competition 2008


*Passion Flowers* and *Coming to Prague in Winter* were published in Envoi Magazine in 1994

*At the Hope Bay Cafe* and *Sachertorte* were published in 'Kites' Anthology 2008

*The Day of the Shoot* was published in The RADA Poets in 2009

*Piccadilly Circus* and *To Billy Collins* were published in 'Kites' Anthology 2010

*On London Bridge* was published in the South Bank Poetry Magazine in 2011

# Contents

## Country

## Seaside

## City

## Love

## Life

## Death

## War

## Language

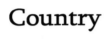

Country

# Bird Farm

The parrots chained on their perches
are silent in the dark outside,
having screeched and squawked all day.
The long lean dogs rest their noses on their paws
just inside the door.

My uncle sits by the paraffin lamp
reading his book,
then suddenly looks up
with his expressionless glare.
His awkward bullet-broken hand
indicates the stairs.

My aunt, on her hard high-backed chair
raises her eyes from silent prayer,
holds out the candle
with her tired smile.
No one speaks.
Upstairs the dark house waits

To take me
as I leave the room.

# Brother Adam and the Bees

They were big black bees
producing honey pot by precious pot,
famous round that part of Devon and beyond.
Brother Adam, in the hours he wasn't contemplating
    Heaven
on his knees (or to be honest, even when he was)
thought about his bees and how to care for them
a lot.
Brother Adam
never left the monastery one single day
in case they should fall ill
or be attacked by some pernicious plague.
Hourly he prayed for them.
Why not?

Sadly one fine and sunny day
his prayers did not reach Heaven.
A bee-destroying disease
swept through Devon, took their lives.
Each one died.
Brother Adam knelt before his hives
and cried and cried.
Then took his greatcloak and his sticks (he needed two)
and crucifix
and set off round the world
to see if there were other big black bees
he could return with to the monastery
to breed and start his hives again.

Ten thousand miles and many years
passed by, and still
he travelled on, this most devout of men,
till in Tunisia at last found six.
Only six. And one of those was ill.
Carefully he carried them back home,
slept with them, fasted and prayed for them
until the hives began to buzz again.
Brother Adam and his big black bees
are famous now.
Pardoned from praying on his knees,
he takes his ease
in the orchard of the monastery in Devon.

And famous too
(is it something in the honey?)
for having reached the hardy age
of one hundred and eleven.

# Consider the Moon

The seedsmen are out tonight
at the full of the moon
flinging the seeds with curving spin
knowing the season and the time are right

Low and red in the sky she hangs
has wicked blood in her
and maybe some beneficence
like nettles left in hedges

The men are naked
as they throw the seeds ahead
hoping the moon will take as innocence
and bless this whitened flesh

They finish sweat-drenched in the sunrise mist
gather their shoes and breeches from the trees
tramp home in the early dew
cloudy morning bodes fourteen fair days

The seedsmen lift their pitchers, drink their ale
lay their heads on mattresses of straw
disturb and spoon their wives to warm themselves
wives who bury horsehair underneath their herbs

But consider the moon she has her ways
waxing or waning she sways her waters
takes no heed of their beliefs or needs
however hard their work or good the seeds

# The Golden Hares of Rathlin

Shapeshifting witches
twitching their cleft upper lips
bidden by tides
and ancient hag-magic

must change into hares
and on rust-furred hind legs
sharing their secrets
at the time of the Ides
dance under the moon

But not all witches
need be wizened to be wise
the golden hares of Rathlin
are shapeshifters too

when they take on human form
they are palest blonde
and their eyes are blue
they are young and beautiful
swift and shy

If I
should ever fall in love again
it will be with a golden hare
under the moon when the dances begin
there on the Island of Rathlin

# Drawing The Line

"The line is mainly intellectual, you see. Such purity.
Three dimensions have a more emotional appeal, perhaps,
though not for me."

After I had run away, been brought home in disgrace,
she had not spoken to me. My grandmother.
Days which were very hard to fill.

We walked the lane to Elder's Field then
as we always did, meaning to or not,
with Smokey, Bob and Choice.

"Outside our garden there is not an ordered world. As you
    now
know. Intriguing, naturally, but hostile, alien.
You were not frightened of it, though, I hope?"

Her voice a novelty, a long-awaited pardon,
now we could both pretend it had not happened.
The trunks of sycamores were raw as brand new pencils.

I nearly told her. Wanted to but had no words: you frighten
    me –
God ... Miss White at school ... and Santa Claus –
their broken promises. Whose rules and bargains lack all
    logic.

But we had come to Elder's Field by then
as we always did, meaning to or not.
So we sat and ate our sandwiches.

She talked of fear. The medievals. Symbols of disorder.
   Harm.
"You can't be scared if you are curious,
knowledge is a kind of magic charm."

Nearby the cows munched steadily, ignored the dogs.
Greyhounds they were, lean
(clean-lined and barely three dimensional).

Suddenly a cow leant over me, brushed my arm
and with its rasping tongue wiped the sandwich from my
   hand.
It was so unexpected I cried out, alarmed.

And then I sensed, at last, that she preferred me intellectual
   too,
considered my emotions worthy only of contempt
so I stiffened the lines of my face into silence.

When we walked back home from Elder's Field
a truce was made and we forgave each other
as we always did, meaning to or not.

# Hidden Landscape

This is it she said
dropping down from the stile into wet grass
He stopped half way over
she had passed him
not waited for his outstretched hand
gone on instead

To know her better he had dared
to ask about her childhood
Not in words she said but I will take you
there where there are woods
and grass and clover
fieldmice and birds it was nice she said

Now she stared ahead
across the field to where the land
ended in mist beyond a fringe of trees
hiding the horizon
She held her breath and then
this is it she said again

Eyes on what exactly
he could not tell
and could not ask
for she had gone beyond him
into the distance of those other times
listening for the skylark
lonely for the years between

But there is nothing here he said
She turned do you not see
it is all here in my bones
the soil and the stones and the bark of the trees
without this landscape I am nothing
this is the childhood heart of me

# The Day of the Shoot

Hearing the front door slam, the boy threw the book down
    on the bed
lay with his hands behind his head and thought about
Keats, immortal birds, and easeful death. Made his decision.

Along the faded flowered carpet purposely he roller skated
across the landing, down the staircase, through the hall,
moving towards the green baize door.

Behind it, there were only spiders and their many cobwebs,
mice, old droppings, and dead ants
around an ancient bag of tainted sugar.

His father was an idiot. No idea of poetry, trying to spoil it
    all.
Told him Keats went shooting little birds out on the heath,
and had written to his brother

"How do you come on with the gun?
Have you met with any pheasants? Bang - smoke and
    feathers"!
Hardly likely, was it? Just his father, lying in his teeth.

Taking off his skates, not to disturb the neglect,
carefully he pushed the door
Hating them for having him at all.

Hating them for leaving him when they went out
shooting at the creatures he revered, expecting
him to join the murder of the harmless.

His scrawny mother dressed to kill,
with chicken feet parched yellow by a foreign hotel
    pool,
hidden in gleaming leather boots.

His father, large and shiny, gesturing with his gun,
laughing loudly with the beaters,
embarrassed by the absence of his son.

From the distant woods he heard each shot
through the clear morning air.
His heart dropped with every dying bird.

What if they got a nightingale, just by mistake?
Nightingales are fairly rare round here, apparently.
Not surprisingly, with idiots let loose.

Putting his roller skates back on, he clumped upstairs
    again,
having gathered what he needed.
Cobwebs and droppings and dead ants

and a bag of tainted sugar.

# To Billy Collins

*(formerly American Poet Laureate)*

You write of cows
with "cold unblinking eyes",
and I am brought up short.
Raise my head from reading,
having an urgent need to disagree.

I praise your poems to the skies
for their beauty and their truth,
will brook no argument.
But this I must refute —
the "cold unblinking eyes".

For I recall my youth
in little chunks and chinks,
as people do, I think,
and I grew up with cows.
Channel Island milkers.

Their eyes were loving,
soft, protective and benign,
soulful, gentle, kind, reflective
with eyelashes to melt your heart.
I laid my face on theirs.

I beg you, don't destroy
this shred of memory,
but think again and write
a line with different adjectives.
You are welcome to use mine.

Afterthought

In another poem you write of "Irish cows"
whose sides are "black and white".
If not Channel Island milkers then,
you may be right and I apologise.

# Visiting Rousseau

The hem of my white dress
like common daisy tips
dipped along the pink dust
of the crushed brick
of his path
up to his door.
Paris had become so hot
and what is more
uninteresting
and I had driven out to Montmorency.
Perhaps I had expected Wisdom to be
squatting at his gate.
At any rate, I thought,
he'll talk to me
in something other than
dull high-pitched platitudes.
I was quite willing to be taught.

On my insistence, then, she showed me in
and stood behind me
in the shifting shadows of his room,
the heavy curtain of her face
which I have seen vivid with trivialities
hung drawn in gloomy folds.
She did not say "I told you so".
She stared out through the hurried half-closed
window, nudging into my mind's eye
her own last scrambling sight of him,

one foot still on the sill,
hand to pursed lip at her.
Now he ran cursing through the woods,
a panic stumbling man.

On his desk where yellow sunlight
thick as wax
melted richly into brown,
flooding over piles of papers,
trickling down into the tiny black ravines
of writing on each page,
his pen-feather lay
still shiny with its undried ink.
His chair flung angled by untidy speed.
I heard the backward scrape of it
echo like some bird call in a clearing
listened to an instant earlier,
implicit insult in the silence left.

On one side piled his work notes
Thumbed and rough
Experiences struck out
Emotions underlined for ever here,
And in a central place, in fairer hand
On sheets of finest white and edged with gold
The sun was striking glints from sky and silver
grains of sand.
Traces of a day's work said and done
all neatly sewn together with a thread of royal blue
and on the other side a few
odd pieces, splashed and soiled.

"He weeps then as he writes" I said
"A paper-stainer of another kind."
The effort fell too short between our thoughts.
She did not say, "But not for me"
as pouting Paris women might
but looked out of the window,
quiet and at ease
despite his clumsy flight.

With no reason to linger now,
still I waited,
thought he might return.
No wish to feel the gravel burn again beneath my
    shoes
the hot drive back to Paris
with such lack of news,
no anecdote embroidered to amuse.
I fingered the wild garlic
thrust unarranged into a little pot.
She did not say "you are a child" but looked
and for the first time hard into my eyes,
surprising what I called my ardent heart
into the knowledge of its own avidity.
Now when his name is mentioned at a friend's
I see again the pity in that look,
feel the same shame
and will not even say I read his book.

# My Aunt Said

"It's dark and damp
but it has a chandelier,"
my aunt said
of her newly acquired home.
I was quite appalled.
I said "Why not buy a house
which is warm and light instead
and have a chandelier installed?"
"It wouldn't be the same,"
my aunt said.

# Incident

It is the time of year
when silver mists haunt the trees
and golden leaves lie thickly on the grass,
when William the long dead
mourning the loss in battle of his arm
wanders in the early dawn
through the music room and
out along the flagstones
where he takes the air
until the air takes him.

Later in the morning
after tea and toast and newspapers,
Ivor, in his warmest sweater,
takes the rake and makes a start
to clear the lawn.
The smell of Autumn pleases him,
the untidiness of trees,
which scatter their debris
like teenagers their bedroom floors,
is more a challenge than a chore,

After some minutes he picks up a glove.
He studies it. It is not one of his.
It is perhaps a riding glove,
a gauntlet, old, well made with leather palm.
Not so much a glove as half a glove, the fingers
torn away or severed. The remains of it
show bloodstains. Suddenly he does not like it,
as though it is a symbol of ancestral harm.
And yesterday, he is quite sure, it was not there.

He drops it where it lay. And finishes,
at least as far as it is ever finished
till every leaf has fallen onto winter ground,
the task he came out there to do.
He is that sort of man.
Back inside the house the scent of coffee
is heralding normality.

# Temptation

"Darling," said Eve,
"look what the snake has given me."
"Great," said Adam, "Oh I say,
now we'll have some fun:
this is what life is all about."
He gave her the spade from his delving,
and thought about the matter
then hurled the apple at her
and when she raised the spade
and clouted it, he caught it
and he shouted
"Out!"

"Darling," said Eve quite gently, "I rather
think that we're
supposed to bite the thing."
"Really?" said Adam,
"what a weird idea."

# Seaside

# At the Hope Bay Cafe

The flatlands are cold
stripped by the wind which crosses them
from the cemetery next to the sea.

In the cafe the waiters stand idle
by their tables
while fat men fast.
Carriers of plague embrace
and old historians grow vague about the past.

Nothing changes much, you say,
leaning on your elbows.
staring into cooling coffee.

The child in the red hat
playing in the doorway
feels the chill of drowned men's dreams,
turns back inside
still singing quietly.

# Man Marks the Earth

Surprised as tideless Greeks
Victorians first viewed the English shores at Ilfracombe,
away from the war in Europe and from moral frailty,
seeking the solace of the sea.

Leading the procession
his father quickly strides away in an enormous hat,
   a wide-awake,
a loose black coat with pockets where a pocket never is,
trousers incorruptible, covered by
thick worsted stockings and great fishing boots.
He has his staff, his hammer, chisel and an oyster knife.

Behind, as muses following Apollo,
come spectacled old men stooping to fill baskets.
Hampered by seaweed, women stroll with shrimping nets
and dainty buckets,
shawls falling to a point
at the back edge of dampened petticoats.
Bonnets, swept off by the wind, roll irrevocably far.
Young fathers drop small shells and skeletons
of little crabs, profusely pink and silver,
or the twisted whitened shape of a thin armed brittle-star
into the held out smocks for children to take home
as private treasure.

An ageless funnel in the rocks, spewing foam,
frames his father in an arc of light,
lemon, purple and viridian.
Capstone spout holes briefly sanctify the man.
"Here" he is shouting, arms upraised, "are your
algae, molluscs and your zoophytes.
Collect your specimens, my friends, examine them,
be scrupulous in detail, honest in record.
Enhance the pleasure of your admiration, study, dig down
    deep."

The boy begins to doubt
all his father's certainty of nature's law.
All that enthusiasm, that respect, the earnest books, the
sound advice,
have wrecked the shore.
Rock basins, once neglected and profound,
their history quiet from long before the Greeks,
profaned and vulgarised,
species beyond recall
carried carefully away into aquaria to die.

# Mr Miller's Mistress

Mr Miller works in an office,
In the department called Stats.
Every day of the week there he sits
with figures at his fingertips
till five of the clock when he puts on his hat.

"He's not a bad chap", the others agree
but they won't go much further than that.
He doesn't go after work to the pub
or with girls from the office to dance in a club:
he'd rather go home to Jack Spratt, his cat,

On to a tube train or sometimes a bus,
herrings for tea in his small Wandsworth flat.
He washes the dishes and puts them away
or back on the table for breakfast next day
and then reads the paper out loud to Jack Spratt.

He washes his clothes in the local launderette
but none of his colleagues know that.
In fact they know nothing at all of his life,
not even if he has a mother or wife
let alone of his beautiful cat.

He's just Mr Miller who sits at his desk
and never joins in office chat.
He doesn't offer and they don't expect
anything warmer than mutual respect.
He's not one (like Jack Spratt) for chewing the fat.

But before you regard Mr Miller as sad
or his way of life makes you sigh
I think that I really must tell you this.
He is not altogether a stranger to bliss
and I've no wish to gossip but I'll tell you why.

Mr Miller has a mistress in a beach hut by the sea,
and she's bouncy and she's buxom and blonde as can be.
She smiles at Mr Miller and shakes her wild curls,
her name is Jane Shirley but he calls her "Shirls"
and she loves Mr Miller inordinately.
And from Saturday morning till late Sunday night
they laugh and make love and play games and get tight
and they walk on the sand in the moon's lambent light
and they take off their clothes and rejoice in the sight
and Jack Spratt follows on, his tail high with delight
and everything, everything in their world is right.

# Passion Flowers

He gives her coffee as she likes it
very sweet and strong
does not question what is clear in her

and she is fair
and elegantly dangerous
and she will one day wade into the sea
where soft white waves will fall
and tumble her in mockery

and he will tend the passion flowers
along the sun-cracked wall
and lacking danger
take no care at all

# A Suitable Shell for Treatment

When we took our tortoise down to Brighton for the week
He had a nervous breakdown, wouldn't smile and wouldn't speak.
By which I mean that all communication quite broke down
and yet he'd been so cheerful back at home in Camden Town.
He turned his back and stuck his chin out up against the wall,
no ambling round and certainly no coming to our call.
He wouldn't eat except for snails which he spat out again.
He seemed to have forgotten he was vegetarian.
He didn't want his favourite lettuce even though home-grown,
all he did was fill a space and imitate a stone.
Some people gave us the address of a psychiatrist he could see.
Our mother said we hadn't got the money for the fee.
Of course it spoilt the holiday, it brought our spirits down,
and so we cut our losses and went home to Camden Town.
We put him in the garden, set him carefully on the lawn.
He peered about in disbelief and then he gave a yawn
and off he rambled down the path full of the joys of Spring,
looking back as though suggesting we'd imagined the whole thing.
Now we're very fond of Brighton and the place is sadly missed.
But you can't enjoy your holiday with your tortoise round the
    twist.

# Essouria Then and Now

Sand stung our faces with relentless meanness
as we hit the beach
making me suddenly remember the place.
It hadn't changed
We had reached Essouria as previously arranged
driven across from Marrakesh.

The couple who had shared our car
sitting by Mohammed in the seat up front
hadn't said one word to him,
only grumbled loudly every time we stopped,
regretting Eastbourne.

They took one look at Essouria
and their shower room
and ordered Mohammed
deigning from necessity
to speak to him
to return them there and then
to Marrakesh.

They could not see why we would want to stay
even when a graceful girl
began to pattern petals
in the courtyard fountains.
There was no way we were going to say
to people we didn't want there anyway
"You should have been here in the sixties."
There was no place for them in our sixties,
least of all in Essouria.

Our method of arrival had been different then,
backpacks and a smattering of French
were all the comforts
we had looked for
and a place to sleep.
This French kid
in a club in Frith Street called Le Kilt
had said "You must go to Morocco."
So we did.

Meeting The Crow, as he was known,
Austin Crowe, his real name was,
ex public school boy, and Fat Sam
on the long beach
where the alizee blows strongly,
the place to sleep
was quickly found

Everyone slept at Claude and Pamela la Courbet's place.
Plenty of
well, mattresses laid out, thirty at least
over three floors, round a central courtyard
where our cases stood today
waiting to be taken to our rooms.
Now it's a hotel with some, a few, mod cons
though not enough for the gloomy pair
we had travelled with from Marrakesh.
Yeah-yeah, Peace and Love.

Jokes abounded round the Two Crows,
one French, one English,
and always into soft nights
music and singing and scented smoke
floated away towards the stars.

Occasionally Jimi H would play guitar for us
when he could be persuaded from his room.
He could smoke, oh, could he smoke.
Not the white gold-banded menthol
of his later days but any old thing.
Well, he was like the rest of us.
Except he was a genius.

We were returning home to start our lives,
drama school. art college, uni,
driving an underground train.
We didn't know, didn't care,
it was all out there for us
sometime, somewhere.

They, the priggish couple in the car,
didn't know it then
and they don't like it now.
There is no place for them in Essouria.
No place for them in our sixties.
Goodbye, Jimi, goodbye Peace and Love.

Let them visit their own memories
in Eastbourne.
Yeah-yeah, Peace and Love.
But there are limits.

# City

# On London Bridge

On London Bridge once stood
a chapel where the monks for luxury
kept a fish pond in a vaulted chamber
down a steep and winding stair.
A large square grated opening
in the starling of the pier.
There, as a blessing, salmon came for years
then less and less
causing the brothers grave distress.

The salmon is particular.
Purity of water an essential need.
Miles downstream instinct tells him to turn back
from a black metropolis.
Tar flow or pig slop
or the smallest drop of blood
will stop him in his watery tracks.

The monks preached piety
but unrepentant sinners
in the upper reaches of the Thames,
throwing the entrails of dead sheep
into its murky deep,
returned the spawning salmon to the sea
and deprived the brothers of their little luxury.

# Piccadilly Circus

## (Eros and the Pleasure Principle)

*Marcuse published 'Eros and Civilisation' in 1955.*
*We had not read it.*
*Larkin published his much acclaimed 'The Less Deceived' in 1955*
*and we had read that.*


The length of Regent Street,
the sweep of it, the elegance of curve,
the wit. Circuses at either end;
an architect who kept his Georgian nerve.

When we first came to London we could sit
in the evening on shallow steps
and worship at the base of Eros
(incorrectly named we now find out).

Taxis surging round, people seeking Fun
emerging from the Underground.

The length of Regent Street,
the life of it, the glamour of its lights,
shops, cafes and bars, side-street pubs:
*Civilisation* at its height.

Men in evening dress smoking cigars
stopping to chat outside their clubs,

London's heart, Piccadilly Circus,
a place to start.
Unseen stars above us in the dark,
we talked of Philip Larkin

in our duffel coats and jeans
with empty pockets.
When we were young
and probably in love.

# Coming to Prague in Winter

Searching for the colour of her hair,
shape of her face
since he has not forgotten them
this city constantly evades his eye.
Here all is pale as tallow, moveable as dust.

She says that if he loved her
he would not have come to Prague
without her. She is wrong.

Here, Berlioz, waking in the night
wrote the song of the angelic choir
forgetting many things about Estelle
including the colour of her hair,
shape of her face.

And yet still loved her till she was,
at seventy or thereabouts,
a grandmother
and marriage still discussed.

# Fragment

Ochre, amber, ash façades fade and crumble
just at the moment when the head is turned away.
Courtyards and gardens
fold back in shade behind their walls.
Shadows shift as shutters close when evening falls.
Old rust pits the ironwork,
fountains tumble quietly into moss and mould.
An ancient city grieves, tries to hide itself.
It keeps its secrets though I have loved it so.

But I have loved you too and that is why
tomorrow I must leave.

# Sachertorte

The ground floor tearoom, Sacher's restaurant.
"Not downstairs," my friend says, shoots his cuff, icing
   white,
checks the immaculate jacket of his suit for fluff.
"It has to be the ground floor."
Obviously, because it's packed.
Candles in brackets with small lampshades
against scarlet walls.
Three marbled tiers of sachertorte.
The service is phenomenally slow.
Come on, we're only here a fortnight.

At last we are seated at the farthest end
despite my friend's complaint.
Waiter in DJ and bow tie asks us what we want.
Eventually. Peremptorily.
What does he think?
Sachertorte, of course. Just look at it.
Ah, here it comes.
It is dark, rich, thick and jammy
(rather like my friend
but he does not appreciate the irony)
I ravish its last crumbs.

Coming out, we glance off to the right.
A spacious room, tables laid for many,
set apart theatrically by tasselled silken cord.
At a table in the centre, quite alone
sits a little woman, poorly dressed.
Well, let's be honest here, a bag lady, a crone.
Her shoes just touch the floor, plastic carriers
nuzzle up to them like old exhausted dogs.
The waiter, the same one, in DJ and bow tie
hovers over her. Solicitously. Graciously.

"Twice as large a slice as we got."
gripes my friend, uptight and very piqued.
(I feel the fortnight dwindle.)
A famous beauty in impoverished old age, perhaps?
How very Viennese. A Duchess in disguise?
The chef's eccentric grandmother?
Or in off the pavement
at the waiter's whim?
Whatever, Sacher's tearoom regains my esteem.
Catching the waiter's eye, I grin at him.

# City Lights Blues

### (for Jack Kerouac)

*Tryna get to sunny Californy. Boom.*
You bet your ass.
English middle class Fifties
was a grey faced drag.
Believe me.

Flowered wallpaper and a bed
candlewick spreaded.
Not *an owlish old room*
*to bend over words in*
Though I did.

261 Columbus Avenue
became the dream
and the Cameo Hotel.
You holed up, hiding out,
riding the blues.

*Wham, wham.*
Bardic, this is what I am
Write what comes into your head.
Speak directly to the people.
Middle class poetry is dead.

Have to say
'fraid not, Jack.
Over a caffe amaretto
Here in the Vesuvio bar
Hard to admit the candlewick lives on.

Love

# First Love

At fifteen
you had a brand new camera
and viewed the world through it.
At fourteen
I had a ballerina dress
with three net petticoats.

We walked into the field beyond the house
I posed on a five-barred gate.

and then
we paused
and clicked.

# Fairground Romance

At the annual fairground
the man on the dodgems
(my dream man)
holding onto the poles
at the back
swung from car to car.

Every year I rode with him
ecstatically.
Flashing lights, loud music,
his hands on my shoulders.

The fourth year my father found out.
Knocked his teeth in.
He fell under a car
and was crushed.

Now he has a burger van,
my father's dead,
and I'm too old for dodgems.
Sad, really.

# He Likes, I Like

He likes the Beatles and Beethoven
I like Mozart and Momma Cass
We met at a Madness concert.

He likes De Vinci and photographs of tigers
I like Rembrandt and Greek vases
We met at a Bacon Exhibition.

He likes Erazerhead and Elvira Madigan
I like The Third Man and Cousin Cousine
We met at a rerun of Dumbo.

He likes to fall asleep at four a.m.
New York neon blinking on his eyelids
I like to rise as the stars fade
along the Wye Valley.
We met in Barnsley
at midday.

He likes me,
I like him.
But we've had to stop meeting.

# Hot Night

There is no doubting
the world hurts.
Forest fires flame and scorch,
volcanoes erupt and scald.

Above us stars burn out.
So does love:
we carry the scars.

The night is hot.
She leaves without
washing the dinner plates.
He has hidden the car keys.
A small girl cries in her cot
woken by shouting.

# What to Say

Her hair as bright as copper filings,
the smell of sun-bleached wood and burning brick,
of moon daisies, silk-fescue and juniper.
Flattening the grass they could not wait.

And then the years between.
An amaranthine voyage
or brief as the shrug of a shoulder.

This afternoon
a cold sun lies across the bed
finding no disorder in the sheets.
Sadness settles quietly as dust
and in the distant street
A child calls their goodbye.

# The Letter

He trawls through his morning post
which now arrives as late as half past four
looking for a letter from his wife.
Is there an envelope with her exuberant scrawl
as though a spider had dipped all eight legs in ink,
with his name, unlike its owner, big and bold,
the address in Florentine flourishes
way above its sidestreet status?

If he turns it over
will there be a private coded message on the back
and exes for kisses
as when they wrote
those years ago
their daily teenage notes?

And, on opening, will it ask
"How is Pinkie – have the fleas cleared up?"
or "Has the rose bush any flowers yet?"
or "Has the man been round to clean the windows?"
or even "and how are you, my darling?"

He places the letter, unopened,
on the hall table, takes off his coat.
He'll have a drink, make dinner. Relax
before he tackles what he knows will be
her packed itinerary.

With not a line to say when she'll be coming home
or that she misses him.

# Haunting John Keats

This is my house now.
I have lived here all summer,
looked through your windows,
opened your doors,
listened for your silent nightingale.
I have fallen in love with you,
living today in yesterday.
Sitting in your basement kitchen
I have eaten mozzarella and tomato
just to taste the basil hidden there
and waited for you on St Agnes Eve
beneath the lost plum tree.
I am your Belle Dame Sans Merci.
This is my house now
and you belong to me.

# Crying On the Hard Shoulder

It is dark and wet.

Passing vehicles spray the nearside
of my clapped out Ford.
Crystals shower my window
in oncoming lights,
fall, too, down my cheeks.

CD's on the back seat,
the ones he said were his,
spilling from the rack
onto the floor.

I've phoned the breakdown people.
Appropriately named.
They've seen it all before.
They'll send some men, a tow,
it will be an hour or so.

I could seal the doors,
fill the car with tears by then.
Drowned white face floating,
fish mouth catching crystals.

# Alone

At the time when the tides go down
and the turn of the night is past,
a pale mist creeps beneath
the prowling fox, the owl in flight.

I stand at the window
like my own ghost,
on the bed are our soft white sheets.
Now that you are not here with me
I fade into the light.

# Amour Propre 1926

The cool conservatory heaves
its green glass leaves
at anger carried in
white hot from dancing

In an ice-cream frock
she stops
camellia pale her breasts
and stocking tops

Any girl who has his name down on her dance card
    list
especially for the tango
is asking to be kissed
and hard. An offer few refuse.

He follows
with a dancer's grace.
Come. Where's the harm?
"I do not choose -"

Alone behind the drooping palms
her sudden hand across his waxy face.
His patent hair and shoes
and rage are black

And in this place
near plants which trap the passing fly
he wishes he could crush her for that slap
snap, crunch and swallow she would die.

She moves into the garden
rather bored
and flirts a little
with the stars and sky.

# Twilight

*I have explained the twilight, admittedly
but is it enough?* — Waiting for Godot

Paper lanterns
                    hang
in the emptied garden,
the sun no longer high
above the horizon,
light spilling from the sky.

A harsher light
                    spills
welcome through the house,
particular attraction,
fondness, liking and affection,
ecstasy and passion.

Lover of twilight
come in if you still want to.

# The Waiting

Old fingers lift the lid
the peach glass bowl stands open now for swansdown
squares of sandalwood from Marrakech
lie scentless beneath underwear

ancient training lingers
pulls antique rings over disintegrating bones
and carefully powders the back of each hand

In the room below he stands quite still
among the other relics of her past
staring at her unloved garden
waiting for her as he always has

and always will

# A Short Poem

All the men Miranda met
whose feet were not of clay
Ran away!

# Life

# An Excellent Cure for the Spotted Fever

*(found poem—except the bits in brackets)*

Take of senna, hermodactis, turpethum and scammony.
Take of zedoary, scurvy-grass, orach, mugwort roots.
Take of scordium, galingal, pellitory of the wall.
Take of alkermes, dried millipedes
(first chop them small).

Take of mithridate, filipendula, heira-picra, woodlice.
Of this last at least a hundred boiled in milk.
Take of a peck of snails, oxmel of squills
Take of elecampane, jalap, camphire and crude opium
(form into pills).

Take a pennyworth of black soap, one of gunpowder and
    snuff.
Take of rosin, pound and sift it.
Take of hog's lard and a pinch of pitch,
Take one scruple each of melilot and fanicle
(to cure the itch).

Take of tormentil, lignum aloes, assa foetida and dittany.
Take two drams of agaric, with brimstone flour
Take of mouse dung beaten into powder, carduus –

(By now your patient will quite probably be dead
or wishing that he was.)


Taken from *The Compleat Housewfe or Accomplished Gentlewoman's
Companion* Published in 1758

# Sudden Memory at the Breakfast Table

I had two horses
powerful prancers, beautiful and bold.
I rode them
over mountains, deserts, seas and stars and clouds,
when I was eight years old.

They were a chestnut and a grey.
I followed where they led
and I had found them names of legendary splendour
One was called Golden Syrup
and the other Silver Shred.

# The Present

She was very old, we children thought
What could she want or need?
Not chocolates, they're too boring
so we took her our centipede

(wrapped up in silver paper)

# Our Old White Cat

Our old white cat
is piled up
like a snowdrift
at our back door
he is dying
we are told
of kidney disease
and that is that

already I am thinking
of the day
when a snowdrift
is piled up
at our back door
like
our old white cat

# Our New Black Cat

This cat
was willed to me
by a malevolent old aunt.
He hisses at me, spits and scratches,
sits on my window sill
and glares at me.
and I stare back.
Locked in combat
we dare each other
to die first.

# Small Protests

Now Toad
Martini in my hand
I've looked at you again
Out in the middle of the muddy road
You look so
How to put it kindly
Well, so glum.

Through the window
Of my cheerful room
I looked an hour ago
Since then
I've read the news
The book reviews
Made a stew
Mended a fuse
Sent for a man to do the flues
In fact I've been of use
I've got things done
Have not sat sunk in gloom
Like you

Shall we arrange to take each others place?
Pull each others face until winds change?

If I lay pulsing in the road
Emitting carefully elected belches now and then
I should not be much loved
Don't think I wouldn't like it
Being drunk is great
But here the line that women walk is very fine
Men like us fuddled and affectionate
They hate prostrate
What they had hoped supine

And what of you, with flour on your forehead
Floral overalled or rubber-gloved?
I think the men who all depend on me
Would be appalled, to say the least, offended
What beastly Beatrix Potter trick is this, they'd cry

No, it would be unwise to try
We are both doomed
You swell and bellow on, my friend
And I'll throw ornaments against the wall
We will make small protests, you and I
You in a muddy puddle hell and rather wet
I merry with Martini, very dry.

# To My Daughter

I hold your slender hands
Which weeks in hospital have made so beautiful
Despair in fingernails has turned to vanity
I am delighted by your smallest vanity

And seeing in a bowl beside your bed
Amongst the apples and the yellow flowers
A pomegranate, favour of a friend
I put it in the basket at my feet with nothing said

In some small way this summer I have wandered Hades
Not felt much need to sleep or wash or feed
But I am not possessed of powers to set the earth at odds
Or bargain seasons with the gods
And so you shall not eat one seed

# Felled

The giant I remember stalked among his orchard trees
Pushing me in the wheelbarrow, grit biting at my knees.
He would stop and smile
Take out a tiny pocket-knife
Peel and halve an apple for me.
Sometimes he would pass a penny through my stomach
His hands were wonderfully intelligent
"The Magic Circle," he would say, mysteriously.

He now sits upright lightly on his chair.
Weighs so little.
I have just pushed him round the grounds.
I hold the knotted hand which once had held the world
   for me
Waiting for some magic.

# Arabia

Day
after day
the Arabian sky is blue.

Beyond where the Hindu gardener stoops over a flower
he feeds his father's love birds, Jules et Jim,
collects the post on his way back.
The sand the child has shaken off his naked feet
inside the house holds the heat
more than an hour.

Reading the letters his mother's face is bright
then her shoulders droop.
Sitting staring at her wrists
she knows she will not sleep
for thoughts of misty mornings on the Quantock hills.
England is so green she says to him.
His father sorts through useless newspapers
though he has grown to like his news as history.
Among some bills he opens a manila envelope,
buries his desires desert deep
mourning already his Arabian nights.

Feeling a breath of home
his mother is revived,
Orders by post thick sweaters for her son,
woollen socks
and unforgiving shoes
which not one grain of sand could penetrate.
They will stop with Auntie Kate
until another posting comes his father's way.
If ever.

In the playground, staring
at the alien extra digit on his hand
they surround him, call him fucking freak.
England is grey and full of doubt and miserable little streets

Day
after day
the Arabian skies are blue.
Arabs believe
To have an extra finger on your right hand
signifies good luck.

# Different Views on Art

The paintings were stacked up in the hall
"Putting all that old stuff back, are you?
Seems a shame," said the decorator as he left.
"But it would be sad to be bereft of so much beauty."
The decorator sniffed, quite unconvinced
as grandfather's smile gently closed the door on him.

So back up they went,
every inch of newly gleaming white
covered by murky night scenes or sad dead game
or the dim turbulence of ancient naval fires.
And with each one grandfather's heart rose higher.

# The Romance of Italy

Taggiasca, Pinolina and Merlina
from Western Liguria – Valle Arroscia and
    Valle Lerrone
Coratina, Ogliarola Barese and Leccino
from Largo Gioia del Colle
Moraioio and Frantoio
from Valnerina.
Tonda di Cagliari, Bosana and Neri di Gonnos
Biancolilla,
and Dolci di Rossano from the Piana di Sibari

Wonderful, wonderful.
And I don't even *like* olives.

# Boot Making

At twelve years old it was hard on the hands,
the boot making. If we didn't concentrate
vicious threads cut our fingers.
No tears allowed so none were shed.
No talking, lingering or stopping,
very little earned and fined for being late.

From six thirty till six thirty
hunched over a bench.
nothing was learned but the making of boots.
A bowl of cabbage soup for lunch.
The leather strained against us
not wanting to be sewn or shaped.

But it was all that we had ever known
and marriage at sixteen mistaken for escape.

# Death

# The Obituary

The obituary reads
"He passed quietly in his sleep."
And I think to myself
how strange a thing to die sleeping
or to sleep dying.

We do not sleep through birth,
we struggle for air,
let it be widely known that we are here.
Sometimes slapped
to howl us into life.
An altogether rowdier affair.

So how can we just lie and die
silently and still, unknowing.
The most serious event of our life
and we are not aware,
are not involved in it.

No famous last words, no final yell,
no crying "I want to live!" or "I forgive",
No movement of a hand
in frail farewell.
Slipping in one unrecognised last breath
from sleep to death.

How strange a thing to die sleeping
or to sleep dying.

# Lie of the Land

In the early dawn we stood among the apple trees
in the long wet grass, holding hands.
For two years we have almost talked.
Surviving on the drug of lies,
you were hoping that I did not grieve.

       In the fields beyond the sagging fence
       ghosts marched, sad and dirty remnants
       of a Roman army, not used to failure,
       making the corn sway rhythmically.
       And I knew then that you would leave.

In the afternoon the doctor came,
his small black bag, unremarkably it seems,
holding the bitter pills of illness,
the blinding bandages of death.
As two years bled away, you'd made no sign

       You might have been a soldier, wary
       hoping for an enemy to take the blame
       looking down at sandals darkened by
       dank grass, your eyes were hedged about
       and sorrowful, avoiding mine.

Lifting your head, you escaped to birds.
I did not make a lover's move
nor say your name. And that I think was
wisely done, no time for love now,
best to leave the words unsaid.

> In the dusk we stood again,
> twisted apple trees drip-fed the grass.
> You'd laid your plans so carefully.
> We felt the Roman army pass and pause
> counting their wounded and their dead.

Not knowing if their silent arms enfold,
or severed hands still hold,
quietly we walked, the two of us
down fading washed-out paths
where Roman bones belong

> and words would always have been
> wrong

# Sfumato

Unmoving, right hand
folded over left wrist
and a faint smile.
Who do you remind me of?

Sitting where you have been placed
to face another day.
The bed is crisply made,
no quick return to comfort there.
I sit across from you in silence
studying you as a painter might.

Your robe is neatly tied.
Is it that most beautiful of colours
which Leonardo so much loved,
Dry Turkish Rose?
Is it the masculine rich sunset pink
only the Signoria were allowed to wear?
Or the blush tinted hose with fancy trimmings
Da Vinci bought for his servant
the sly Salai?

The mind wanders when there is nothing to say.

That so subtle sfumato,
layer over layer of shadow from Leonardo's brush
which gives the Giaconda's face its mystery,
has now slipped over yours,
a merging of the edges at the eyes and lips,
in your case from the brush of time.
Your shadows deepen as they lengthen
in the mystery of approaching death.
Not even painters master that.

# Taking Tea

Once every month I walk down this road in Oxford
on the outskirts of the town. Very long.
At its beginning I see its end.
To take tea with an old friend.
She is lame and cannot venture out.
Since the road is unmade, rough and stony.

She could be sad, no doubt, for she is gently dying
yet you would not know. Her eyes are wicked.
She is bright and witty
and every time I go
she makes me feel I am the same.
We have known each other since pramhood.

Every month I tread the path
and note its changes.
Sometimes there is a field on my right
where solitary people walk their dogs;
at other times it is a lake,
Oxford lying so low.

Today the trees have all been pollarded,
Their amputated limbs stretch out to me
as if for help.
I tell them it is for their good
that soon they will recover.
And think again about my friend.

Half way along I pass the playground
just as a class is released to run about and shout.
One small boy, though, does not join the rest
I hear him say to something in his hand
"I shall take you home and give you to my fish."
What, I wonder, would a fish be grateful for?

We are not idiots, my friend and I.
As we take tea and talk and eat her home-made cake
we know that there is war, famine and disease,
tsunami, hurricane and flood,
that the greed, prejudice and cruelty of the world
undermine the good.

And so we speak of the trees
and the boy and his fish
and embrace and wish each other well
until, we hope, next month.

# For Ann

And walking, maybe,
by the sea
or talking in the
candlelight
there you will be.

And as we speak your name
we will reach out,
not now to touch your hand
but to remember how we were.
And you, who always did,
will understand
that neither dancing wave nor flame
could make our eyes this bright.

War

# November 1918

With the pausing of the guns
he waited
heard not silence but the frogs
melancholy hecklers in the mudpools
out beyond the trench
by the group of wooden crosses
out beyond the cartridge cases
empty soup tins.
Out beyond his private stench.

Just a lull the rumour said.
Hold on boy. Don't wonder what to do,
don't imagine it's the end.
Don't start to fraternise with Fritz,
it's just a ploy.
But it was eerie, hearing only frogs.

Later, hours later, he was told
the war was done,
remembered days like this at home
when he and friends
had thrown stones in the village pond
at frogs in fun.
Had not known then
that even frogs die, not in fun,
but seriously, quite meaning it.

# Famous Photograph

The book, a present,
sits, as its name suggests it should,
smugly on the coffee table. Famous Photographs.
It is late afternoon. The lamps are lit.
The boy plays safely on the fireside rug.
I pick the book up, casually open it.

He comes to see and reaches for a hug,
puts his cheek against my face,
and I must take him on my knee
to show my child his world.
Try to explain to him
the photograph the book has chanced to open at.

He laughs.
"Look, playing games," he says
and, soft-nailed, points.
She runs for ever, arms raised, naked, down that
dusty road.
"No, not a game." I say
and frighten him with too tight an embrace.

# Today

From the newspaper I learn that she lives now in Toronto.
Caught by a camera again, she is reported saying,
"I am happy, I forgive.
I live without hatred for what happened then."
It gives their names, Kim and Thomas.
The little boy raises his arms to the bubbles she has blown.
She has her own son now
and they really are playing games.
It is a joyful image, filled with love and fun.

Raises his arms.

and still I am not comforted.

# Most of Us

Most of us
If asked
And of course we're not
Simply want
To be left
In peace

We don't go
Making bombs
In our basements
Most of us

Most of us
When told
Do what is required
Given that
The order's from
Above

We don't go
Hurting folk
Unless we must
Most of us

Most of us
At heart
Want to do what's right
Just so long
As it's con-
Venient

We don't go
Making waves
Out of turn
Most of us

And we shall die surprised wondering what the noise was
Most of us

# Watching the Television Sunday November 8th

Sunday morning
slight rain
crushed underfoot
bright leaves fall
into the mud

hundreds march
or cannot march
holding their memories
millions of unseen ghosts
between

I see the Queen in close up
standing still and stiffly at attention
trying not to cry
because she is the Queen
but I can mourn
and freely weep
for all the dead
and for the not yet born
whose lives will end in
an untimely death
or mutilation

stupid stupid senseless
sodding stupid
bloody stupid sodding bloody war

# Language

# I Have

I have
of late
And wherefore
I know not

Taken to talking
only in
Shakespearean verse
and verily

Methinks
it serves me well
except when
ordering pizza and chips

# Arrivederci

She was Italian
and a lovely woman
We used to chat at the street corner
but she never quite got the hang
of the English language.

She would say "I turned the light on
and the whole room was eliminated"
or "I heard it in the grapeyard"
adding that the rumour had spread
"like wildflower".
She really was a poet.

She told me her daughter-in-law
was not a careful cook,
was a bit slapstick.
I imagined a menu of custard pies
and the odd string of sausages.
She had painted her sitting room, she said,
"with a rather dark emotion".
Gloom, I presumed.

One day she told me she had discovered
"many old Muscovites" in her cellar.
She really meant Muscatel (bottles of)
I was pleased for her,
so much more useful than a load of
ancient Russian layabouts.

On the afternoon she said goodbye
she told me she was moving.
I asked her why.
"Ah" she said sadly
"somebodys at my husband's factory was axed
and men were hacked off
and then everybodys got put in the sack".
I said it sounded... dreadful.

Later I missed her.
Missed the courage of those headstrong
headlong lunges
at the English tongue.

# Our Local Poet

This morning I met, bumped into almost,
our local poet
in his cloak and broad brimmed black hat
taking one of his rare breed stanzas for a walk
I asked if he could let me have a sonnet or two
to tide me over.

Poets should never be mean.
Only last year I lent him a sestina
which he has never given back.

Surely some verse form or other
is burning a hole in his pocket
an octet or quatrain or even a measly couplet
to help me out, when rhymes are hard.

Sale or return then
I suggested
Are you mad he shouted
Striding away

# Triolet

I swear I'll tame the triolet
Try to escape me though it might.
I'll struggle with it night and day,
I swear I'll tame the triolet.
It will not get away this time,
I'll trap it in its own damn rhyme .
I swear I'll tame the triolet
Try to escape me though it might.

I knew I'd get it wrong again
It's driving me quite mad.
Although I know I'm not insane,
I knew I'd get it wrong again.
So there is nothing I can add,
My triolet is really bad.
I knew I'd get it wrong again
It's driving me quite mad.

# This Is Not a Poem

I would write a poem for you, find the words,
search out a thesaurus to look for them.
Arrange long journeys on a country bus
to sit and think about their ordering.
If that was what it took.

No need for that: the words are there.

Lark-lyric filled, hay-making high and blown about with butterflies,
the meadow of my poem could be overgrown with
    wild and sweet-stemmed words
or phrases drunk with love as bees with
    nectar on a foxglove crawl.

And that's the problem, after all.

It comes too strangely strongly in the English tongue,
is somehow wrong;
I need expression which is not absurd,
subtle yet in which some art is found:
    language of the middle ground.

But poetry goes mad, so I can only say:

I would write a poem for you, find the words,
search out a thesaurus to look for them.
Arrange long journeys on a country bus
to sit and think about their ordering.
If that was what it took.

# On the Verandah

They sit outside on her verandah,
light chinking from their wine,
on elegant wrought iron chairs.
Not comfortable for him as it turns out
He is too unfashionably built for them.
Her hair falls back, sleek and silver
as she tilts her face towards the blue-black sky.

"I should like to die out here," she sighs
"with the moonlight harsh and melting in my bones
like love."

He thinks about his wife at home,
Head bent over the kitchen table
making lists:
Take kitten to the vet
Lawn seed
Dentist
Oven fries.

And suddenly knows
what is wrong with this woman
On the verandah:
She is desperately
Overwritten.

# Cannery Row

It's Monterey, California.
We're sitting on a low wall
backs against billboards
we're eating cinnamon muffins
in the thin but kindly sunshine.
A metre from our feet
a cat lies on the sidewalk
cleans its paw, parting one claw at a time.
Content, perhaps she has a slippery silvery
salivatory race memory of sardines
and a trace of Steinbeck's loving heart.

# Prospero's Cell

It's Kassiopi, Corfu.
You should have been here thirty years ago
the old people say to us.
they may be right.

They said it
when we first came here to Kassiopi
and I first read this book
on our return reopened now.
Crushed dry between its wrinkled pages
twenty seven species of wild flower
collected thirty years ago.

*In the tinkling of teacups,*
*the croon of doves, the creak of cicadas*
*the sigh of bats at dusk,*
Durrell sat and wrote about the sky
   *amber and lemon*
   *ink blue and silver.*

Sixty years ago he wrote this book,
his love song to the island,
and yet it is still here, the sky
   amber and lemon
   ink blue and silver.
Old people can be wrong.

# Mayonnaise, Possibly

Mayonnaise
Is mystery
Its history
Obscure
Grimod de la Reynière
Thought it might be
Bayonnaise
Or Mahonnaise
He wasn't sure.
But Bayonne
It is thought
And Mahon
(The Fort
Captured by Richelieu)
Are just *un peu*
Lacking in (and as)
A local sauce.
We could, of course,
Refer to
Magnonaise
from the old verb to stir
Till the year of
Eighteen sixty
It was so.
Like Grimod de la Reynière
We do not know.
The recipe remained throughout the same
Pedants, not gourmets, fret about the name.

# Gertrude's Lost Speech

**Hamlet** Act 3 Scene 1
*Exeunt Rozencrantz and Guildenstern*


Gertrude:

Now hath he caught moon madness
And howls as wolves and wandering spirits do
Into the midnight air.
Now are his courtly manners mantled o'er
And sorrow bends the sweetness of his speech.
Did I not warn him from the battlements
When he was but five years on life's path?
Did I not tell him to beware of heights
To feel the fear not only of the fall
From cloud to solid earth but of the mind
From that same earth to passion filled void?
The virtues learned in Wittenberg are lost
The wits deranged by visions of the dead
And wiser lessons from a mother's knee
Forgot. So climbed he on the battlements
And what will come of it, we're yet to see.

In Memory of Marcel Marceau

# Notes

# Notes
## to a few of the poems

Bird Farm

Sometimes as a child I went to stay with an aunt and uncle who owned a farm. It was a proper farm but my aunt also raised exotic birds, hence the name. The farmhouse was very old, without gas or electricity.

The Golden Hares of Rathlin

The hares that live only on the Island of Rathlin have a unique form of albinism that makes them pale but does not affect their eyes.

Drawing the Line

My maternal grandmother brought me up from the age of four until I was twelve. She was a martinet but I adored her.

The Day of the Shoot

I wrote this after reading Keats' letters. In fact the boy in the poem is wrong: Keats really did write those things in his letters to his brother.

Visiting Rousseau

Rousseau fled to the country to avoid the Parisian women who lionised him. This one won't give up!

Piccadilly Circus

The statue is in fact that of Anteros, the god of mature, requited love, rather than, as is commonly thought, that of his brother Eros, the god of physical, erotic love.

| | |
|---|---|
| Sachertorte | The place, the cake and the old lady are real, "my friend" a figment of poetic licence. |
| City Lights Blues | In 2000 I went with my daughter on the trail of the Beat poets and ended up in Columbus Avenue, San Francisco. |
| Haunting John Keats | In 2001 I was appointed Poet in Residence at Keats House, his former home in Hampstead. This is my farewell ode to the great man on leaving the house. ' |
| To My Daughter | At age sixteen, my daughter spent a long time in hospital. A reference to Demeter and Persephone in Greek mythology. |
| Famous Photograph and Today | These should be taken together: then and now. The photograph of the 'Napalm Girl' – nine-year-old Kim Phuc – by Nick Ut was taken at the village of Trang Bang in on 8 June 1977 and was instrumental in changing public opinion in the United States to the Vietnam War. |
| Gertrude's Lost Speech | Like many actresses who are privileged to play this part, I felt short-changed by Shakespeare. Here is my attempt to make amends on his behalf. |